Sarah Tyson Heston Rorer

New Salads for Dinners, Luncheons, Suppers and Receptions

With a group of odd salads and some Ceylon salads

Sarah Tyson Heston Rorer

New Salads for Dinners, Luncheons, Suppers and Receptions
With a group of odd salads and some Ceylon salads

ISBN/EAN: 9783337243807

Printed in Europe, USA, Canada, Australia, Japan

Cover: Foto ©Lupo / pixelio.de

More available books at **www.hansebooks.com**

NEW SALADS

FOR DINNERS ✌ LUNCHEONS

SUPPERS AND RECEPTIONS

With a group of ODD SALADS

and some CEYLON SALADS

❧

By MRS S T RORER

Director of Philadelphia Cooking School
and Author of Mrs Rorer's Cook Book
Canning and Preserving and various other
works on Cookery ● ● ● ●

Published at Philadelphia by

ARNOLD AND COMPANY

Printed at the Sign of the Ivy
Leaf in Philadelphia by George
H Buchanan and Company

ETTUCE and cress have, from the earliest times, occupied a most prominent place among the dinner salads. We are told that the Hebrews ate them without dressing, simply sprinkling over them a little salt. The Greeks, however, used honey and oil, while the Romans served lettuce with hard-boiled eggs, oil and spice, making a salad much more to the liking of the present generation. These salads, however, were served as the first course. They were considered a great luxury, and probably appetizers, as in those days foods were heavy and were served in enormous quantities.

A salad made from a succulent green vegetable and French dressing should be seen on the dinner-table in every well-regulated house three hundred and sixty-five times a year. These green vegetables contain the salts necessary to the well-being of our blood ; the oil is an easily-digested form of fatty matter ; the lemon juice gives us sufficient acid ; therefore, simple salads are exceedingly whole-some. We do not refer here to the highly-seasoned mixtures of meats and vegetables with a heavy mayonnaise dressing. These are rather objection-able. However, if one omits the mustard, seasoning the materials lightly and sensibly, and serves such salads for a lunch or for an evening collation, they are much more wholesome than the average fried dish, upon which many depend for their fatty food.

During the summer, the dinner salad may be composed of any well-cooked green vegetable, served with a French dressing ; string beans, cauliflower, a mixture of peas, turnips, carrots and new beets, boiled radishes, cucumbers, toma-toes, uncooked cabbage and daintily cooked spinach. In the winter, serve celery, lettuce, endive, chickory, escarole or chervil, which, by the way, is very scarce in the Eastern markets.

The heavy meat salads, those composed of chicken, beef, mutton, veal, fish or shell-fish, mixed with vegetables, are usually served with a mayonnaise dressing. Where one wants a sour salad it is always better to marinate the meat by sprinkling with lemon juice or tarragon vinegar an hour before mixing it with the dressing. If too much vinegar be added to the dressing it robs it of its consistency and best flavor.

The different parts of a salad should not be mixed together or with the dressing until serving time.

SALAD SAUCES AND DRESSINGS

SALAD SAUCES AND DRESSINGS

French Dressing

This dressing, if for a dinner salad, should be made at the table, and is most quickly and easily done by shaking in a bottle. It may, however, and usually is, made in a dish or bowl. Put in first, a half teaspoonful of salt and a dash of white pepper; rub the salad fork with garlic; add four tablespoonfuls of olive oil, and stir with the fork; add one tablespoonful of vinegar or lemon juice, mix well and pour it over the salad.

Italian Dressing

Put into a bowl a half teaspoonful of salt, a quarter teaspoonful of white pepper and a teaspoonful of tomato paste. If you cannot get the paste use a teaspoonful of tomato catsup. The paste, however, is very much better. Add

gradually four tablespoonfuls of olive oil,
mixing all the while.   Cut into small
pieces one clove of garlic ; with the back
of a spoon rub the garlic and the paste
well into the oil ; add one tablespoonful
of tarragon vinegar, beat thoroughly,
strain, and it is ready to use.

If made at the table drain it from the
bowl, holding back the garlic with the
fork.

Mayonnaise Dressing

Put the yolks of two eggs into a clean,
cold, soup dish.   Stir lightly with a
wooden fork, adding a quarter teaspoonful
of salt, which should slightly thicken the
yolks.   Now begin to add, drop by
drop, a half pint of cold salad oil, stirring
rapidly until glossy and thick ; add a teaspoonful of tarragon vinegar and one of
lemon juice, or all tarragon vinegar or all
lemon juice may be added.   This dressing may be used at once, or it may be
covered and kept for several days.

Where a large quantity of dressing is
wanted, put three yolks in an ordinary
good-sized earthen bowl.   Stand this
bowl in a pan of ice water or cracked ice.

Have a quart of oil on the left ; measure four tablespoonfuls of plain or tarragon vinegar, put it in a little cup at the right. Now begin to add the oil just as for a smaller quantity, drop by drop, stirring while adding. After adding the first gill, you may add a tablespoonful at a time, and with it a half teaspoonful of the vinegar, and so continue adding oil and vinegar until you have the desired quantity of dressing, allowing a table-spoonful of vinegar to every half pint of oil used, seasoning with red pepper. Depend upon the salad materials rather than the dressing for the seasoning.

Mayonnaise Dressing with Whipped Cream

Where the flavor of oil is not liked, or where a large quantity of dressing is needed at little expense, after the mayonnaise has been made according to the above directions, stir in one pint of cream, whipped to a stiff froth, to each quart of oil. Make the dressing complete. Then at serving time have ready the whipped cream. Mix and use at once.

Green Mayonnaise

Make a mayonnaise dressing according to the first rule.   Chop very fine sufficient parsley to make one tablespoonful.   Put it in a bowl and rub with the back of a spoon until it is reduced almost to a paste ; add during the rubbing four or five drops of alcohol.   Stir this into the mayonnaise and it is ready to use.

Sauce Tartar

Make a green mayonnaise, and to each gill add one gherkin, a tablespoonful of capers, and four olives chopped fine and a half teaspoonful of onion juice. Use tarragon vinegar in making the mayonnaise.

Mayonnaise with Aspic

When mayonnaise dressing is used for garnishing, it is, as a rule, pressed through a forcing bag containing a star tube. Mayonnaise alone is not sufficiently stiff to remain firm.   That it may be built into any form desired, to add to its beauty, rather than to its taste, a small quantity of aspic jelly is frequently mixed with it.   Where recipes call for special decorations, have ready

the mayonnaise without whipped cream.
To each gill, or half cup, of mayonnaise,
add four tablespoonfuls of cold aspic.
It must be very cold, but not congealed.
After mixing stand it aside until the
whole congeals. Then, if desired, a
small quantity of whipped cream may
be stirred in. Use quickly when put
into the bag, or the heat from the hand
will make it liquid again.

Cooked Salad Dressing

Put the yolks of four eggs, four
tablespoonfuls of olive oil and four tablespoonfuls of water or stock into a bowl;
stand in a pan of boiling water and stir
constantly until the dressing is smooth
and thick; take from the fire and add a
half teaspoonful of salt. Put a slice of
onion, a bay leaf, a quarter teaspoonful
of celery seed and four tablespoonfuls of
tarragon vinegar into a saucepan; stand
this over the fire and evaporate the
vinegar one half; then add the mixture,
a few drops at a time, to the dressing;
strain, cool and it is ready to use.

This dressing is especially nice with
cold boiled fish or with canned salmon,
served with or without lettuce leaves.

Sidney Smith's Salad Dressing

Press one fresh boiled or baked potato through a sieve ; then rub it with a limber knife until perfectly smooth ; add to it the yolk of one egg, rub thoroughly and then add another yolk. Add a half teaspoonful of salt and a dash of cayenne. Now add gradually four tablespoonfuls of olive oil ; then two teaspoonfuls of vinegar or the same quantity of lemon juice, and it is ready to use.

This dressing is greatly improved if it has just a suspicion of onion juice, not more than five or six drops, rubbed on the plate before putting on the potato. It may be used in the place of mayonnaise, and is nice with celery, tomatoes or lettuce.

A Custard Dressing

Put a gill of cream over the fire in a double boiler. Moisten one tablespoonful of corn starch with a little cold milk, add it to the hot cream, stir, and cook until smooth. Add hastily the beaten yolks of two eggs. Take from the fire, and when cool add a teaspoonful of tarragon vinegar, a half teaspoonful of salt and a dash of cayenne.

Milk may be used in the place of cream, and a tablespoonful of butter added when the mixture is taken from the fire.

German Salad Dressing

This dressing is used in certain parts of Germany for a salad composed of apples, potatoes and cold roasted beef.

Put a half pint of bouillon, or good stock, into a saucepan, add a slice of onion, two bay leaves, and a little chopped celery tops ; stand over the fire until it reaches boiling point, and then stir into it a tablespoonful of arrowroot moistened in a little cold bouillon. Cook for a moment, strain through a fine sieve, and add to it the yolks of four eggs, two tablespoonfuls of tarragon vinegar and four tablespoonfuls of olive oil. Whisk with an egg-beater until light, then add a half teaspoonful of salt, a teaspoonful of German mustard, and a dash of cayenne ; stand aside until perfectly cold. Cut three boiled potatoes into thin slices, add to them one tart apple sliced, a half pint of cold roasted beef cut into dice, and one small onion cut into very thin slices. If at hand, cut sufficient celery to make a half pint. Mix together and season with a half teaspoonful of salt, a table-spoonful of lemon juice and a saltspoon-ful of white pepper. Mix with the dressing, serve on lettuce leaves and cover with finely-chopped parsley.

This dressing may be used for other mixtures of meat and vegetables.

Cream Dressing

Put the hard-boiled yolks of two eggs in a plate. With a limber knife, rub them smooth ; add gradually six tablespoonfuls of clarified butter or very thick cream ; when smooth add a table-spoonful of vinegar, a half teaspoonful of salt, and a dash of pepper.

While this is a very homely dressing, not nearly so tasty or wholesome as a mayonnaise, it may be used in an emerg-ency. Is fair on dandelions or wilted sour dock, or shredded cabbage.

NEW SALADS

A GROUP OF DINNER SALADS

Asparagus Salad

Trim neatly one bunch of asparagus; tie the stalks together and stand them in a deep kettle of boiling water. Add a teaspoonful of salt to each quart of water, cover the kettle and cook slowly for forty-five minutes. By placing the asparagus so that the butts only will be in the water the stalks will be more evenly cooked. They will fall when soft, and the remaining time will be quite sufficient for the cooking of the tops. Lift the asparagus from the water, drain and stand aside to cool. At serving time pour over French dressing.

String Beans

Select young, tender beans; cut the strings from both sides. Then cut each bean into three pieces lengthwise, throwing them into cold water as soon as cut. When ready to cook, cover with boiling salted water. Boil for twenty minutes, and drain; throw them into cold water for ten minutes. Then put them into boiling unsalted water and cook fifteen minutes longer. This is the proper method of cooking beans when served as a vegetable. A larger quantity may be cooked than is needed for the dinner, so that a portion may be reserved for salad the next day. Drain the beans after they have finished cooking; arrange them evenly crosswise on the platter; sprinkle two tablespoonfuls of vinegar over them and stand away until cold. When ready to serve cover with French dressing.

Plain Cucumbers

Pare fresh, crisp cucumbers; cut into thin slices; soak in very cold clear water one hour; drain, sprinkle plentifully with French dressing and serve at once.

Lima Bean Salad

Select young lima beans containing a small amount of starch, and cook carefully in boiling salted water for twenty minutes. Drain, throw them on a nap-

kin, and turn from side to side until dry
and cool. Line a salad bowl with lettuce
leaves, put the beans in the centre and
stand them in the refrigerator until cold.
When ready to serve cover with French
dressing, and sprinkle over them a tablespoonful of finely-chopped mint.

Beet Salad

Cut boiled beets into thin slices, and
arrange in a salad bowl that has been
lined with lettuce leaves; cover with
French dressing and serve.

This salad may be served with mayonnaise dressing, cutting the beets into
dice. Sidney Smith's dressing is also
especially nice here.

Cabbage Salad

Cut a hard head of cabbage into
halves, and then, with a sharp knife,
shred very fine the quantity desired.
Throw into ice water as fast as shredded,
and allow it to stand about two hours;
then drain until dry. Turn it into the
salad bowl, cover with French dressing
and serve.

This is a very nice winter salad.

Cauliflower Salad

Wash one head of cauliflower and soak in cold water for thirty minutes. Drain, throw into a kettle of boiling salted water and simmer gently for thirty minutes. The cauliflower must not lose its color; boil slowly to keep perfectly white. When done, take it from the water and break it apart in flowerets; place these on a dish, and stand aside until very cold. When ready to serve arrange on a platter, sprinkle over a little chopped parsley, cover with French dressing and serve.

Philadelphia Cooking School Salad

Pare and chop fine one fresh cucumber, and throw it into cold water. Shred sufficient cabbage to make one pint and throw it also into cold water. Peel one good-sized tomato, cut it into halves, press out the seeds, and then chop the flesh rather fine. Remove the seeds from one sweet pepper, and chop it also; mix it with the tomato. Now drain the cucumbers and dry them. Drain and shake the cabbage. Put into the salad bowl a layer of cabbage, then a layer of cucumber, then tomato and pepper, then a few drops of onion juice, another layer of cabbage, and so continue until you have used all the materials. Cover with French dressing, to which has been added a teaspoonful of onion juice, and serve at once.

Celery Salad

Wash and cut the white celery into slices. Dry it on a towel, turning from side to side until dry. Dish it in a salad bowl, and at serving time, cover with French dressing.

It is greatly improved by having ten drops of Worcestershire sauce added to the dressing.

Chicory Salad

This may be washed, made crisp in cold water, dried and served with French dressing.

Escarole and endive are used in the same way. Coming in the winter, they take the place of lettuce and make the nicest of dinner salads.

Italian salad dressing is especially nice with all these green salads.

Celery and Tomato Salad

Peel six solid tomatoes; cut off the stem ends and remove the seeds. Chop sufficient celery to make a half pint. Put the celery in the tomatoes, and arrange them on little nests of lettuce leaves. Pour over each two tablespoonfuls of French dressing and serve.

Cress Salad

Wash, shake until dry, and serve with French dressing.

Carrot Salad

Cut large, perfect carrots into slices. Then, with a vegetable cutter, cut into fancy shapes. Throw them into unsalted water and simmer gently for one hour; drain, and when cold, dish on lettuce leaves; pour over them French dressing and serve.

Nut Salad

This salad is exceedingly nice to serve with roasted wild or tame duck, or with a game course.

Shell a half pint of English walnuts, keeping the kernels in perfect halves, if possible. Cover with boiling water, boil

for five minutes and then blanch, remov-
ing the skin carefully from all the little
crevices. Put the walnuts into a saucepan ; cover with a pint of stock ; add a
bay leaf, two tablespoonfuls of chopped
onion, a tablespoonful of chopped carrot
and a sprig of parsley. Simmer gently
for twenty minutes and then drain ; stand
away until cold. Chop fine one truffle
and twelve mushrooms. When ready to
serve, line the salad bowl with lettuce or
chickory, cut an orange into halves and
scoop out the pulp. Put this pulp over
the lettuce leaves, then a sprinkling of
truffles and mushrooms, then the walnut
kernels, and then the remaining mushrooms and truffles. Send to the table
with French dressing ; mix and serve.

Orange Salad

This salad should be served with the
game course.

Line the salad bowl with crisp lettuce
leaves, and put over them the pulp from
three good-sized oranges. Rub the bowl
in which the French dressing is mixed
with a clove of garlic. Pour the dressing over the salad and serve at once.

Grape Fruit Salad

This is made the same as " Orange Salad," using one grape fruit to each four persons.

Macedoine Salad

A jar of macedoine, already cooked, may be purchased for this salad ; or turnips, carrots, sweet and white potatoes may be cooked separately, mixed together and then mixed with a few string beans or peas. Serve on lettuce leaves and cover with French dressing.

Macedoine in Turnip Cups

This is one of the most sightly of all the dinner salads. Purchase a jar of macedoine, turn out the contents, drain and stand in the refrigerator until cold. Select six small, sound turnips. Pare them and cut off the root end so that they will stand evenly ; then cut a slice from the stem end, and with a potato scoop, scoop out the inside, leaving the turnip in the form of a cup, with a wall about a half inch thick. Throw these cups into unsalted boiling water. Pull the saucepan to the back of the stove where they cannot boil, but will remain at boiling point for thirty minutes until tender ; then drain them and stand away to cool. At serving time arrange each cup on a little nest of lettuce leaves. Fill it with the macedoine, cover with French dressing and send to the table.

The chokes from the French artichokes may be used in place of turnips.

Russian Salad (Simple)

Line a salad bowl with crisp lettuce leaves. Put over them one or two tomatoes which have been peeled and chopped rather fine. Cover with French dressing and serve.

Spinach Salad

This is exceedingly nice to serve with a salmi of rabbit or with roasted duck. Wash two quarts of spinach and remove the leaves from the stems. Throw these leaves into a large kettle, stand over the fire, shake and toss them for ten minutes until they are thoroughly wilted, then drain dry and chop fine. Pack into small dariole molds or egg cups, and stand in the refrigerator. Cut three or four white turnips into slices, and, with a round cake cutter, stamp them out into rounds about two inches in diameter. Stamp some slices of cold boiled tongue at least a half inch larger. When ready to serve make little nests of the lettuce leaves on a platter. In the centre of each put the round of tongue, on top of this the turnip and turn the little cups of spinach in the centre. Make a mayonnaise dressing unusually stiff by adding aspic, as directed in " Mayonnaise with Aspic." Place this in a pastry bag containing a star tube; press around the base of the molds and put just a little on top as a cap. Serve at once.

LUNCHEON, SUPPER AND RECEPTION SALADS

Salads with Mayonnaise Dressing

These salads should be served either for lunch or supper, or for a cold collation. There are times when a salad with mayonnaise dressing may be served for dinner. The salad portion under such circumstances should be very light, either tomato, celery or lettuce. Do not combine them with fish, fowl or meat.

Chicken Salad

The chicken should be especially boiled for salad and carefully seasoned while boiling. Put it into a kettle of boiling water, add a chopped onion, a tablespoonful of chopped carrot, two bay leaves, a teaspoonful of whole pepper corns, and a half teaspoonful of celery seed. Allow the chicken to boil rapidly for five minutes, then put it on the back part of the stove, where the water will be kept at 180° until the chicken is tender. This will make the dark meat as white as the white. Remove the chicken, and when cold, take the flesh in large pieces, from the bones, rejecting all fat and skin. Cut the meat into dice, measure it; and then cut into the same sized pieces sufficient celery to make two-thirds the quantity. If the salad is not to be served immediately, keep the chicken and celery apart until serving time. Sprinkle a tablespoonful of lemon juice over the chicken before standing away. Make a good stiff mayonnaise dressing; add cream or use plain, as preferred. At serving time garnish the salad bowl with lettuce leaves; mix the chicken and celery together. To each quart add a teaspoonful of salt, a half teaspoonful of pepper, and sufficient mayonnaise dressing to cover every piece. Mix thoroughly and turn into the salad bowl on the lettuce leaves; put over a little extra dressing, garnish the centre with the heart of the lettuce head and sprinkle over a tablespoonful of capers which have been drained dry. Garnish with olives and celery tips.

Chicken and Almond Salad

This is made the same as the Chicken Salad, boiling the chicken as directed in " Chicken Salad," cutting the celery, and mixing with each pint of chicken blocks a quarter pound of almonds that have been blanched and cut into quarters.

Mrs. Rorer's Chicken Salad

Boil the chicken as directed in " Chicken Salad." Parboil a pair of sweetbreads. Cut into good-sized pieces sufficient celery to make the same quantity as of chicken. Blanch a half pound of English walnuts and cook for twenty minutes in stock. Blanch a half pound of almonds and chop them rather fine. At serving time line a platter with crisp lettuce leaves. Mix the chicken, celery, sweetbreads, almonds and walnuts, to each quart allowing a teaspoonful of salt, a teaspoonful of Worcestershire sauce, a quarter teaspoonful of paprica. Mix thoroughly, rubbing first the fork with a clove of garlic. In the centre of the salad bowl under the lettuce leaves put three slices of onion. These are simply to be used as flavoring and not to be served with the salad. Now mix with the salad sufficient mayonnaise dressing to cover each piece, and heap it on top of the lettuce leaves. Put a little more dressing over the top, and sprinkle over one truffle chopped fine. Have blanched and chopped two ounces of pistachio nuts ; sprinkle these over with the truffles and serve at once.

This may also be served in little paper cases, the tops garnished with mayonnaise and aspic—the pistachio nuts sprinkled over, and capped with truffles.

Cream of Chicken Salad

Take the white meat from one boiled chicken, chop it very fine, then rub to a powder. As the meat is put through the chopping machine, chop also twelve blanched and dried almonds. Add to this a teaspoonful of salt, a half teaspoonful of paprica, a teaspoonful of onion juice and four tablespoonfuls of thick mayonnaise dressing. Mix, add two tablespoonfuls of lemon juice and a gill of aspic. Mix again and stand aside

until the mixture begins to congeal. Then
stir in hastily a gill of cream that has
been whipped to a stiff froth. Turn this
into a border mold and stand away for
at least two hours to harden. When
ready to serve cover a flat dish with crisp
lettuce leaves, dip the mold quickly into
boiling water, turn the cream salad out
on the lettuce leaves. Cut sufficient
celery to make a pint, mix it with plain
mayonnaise dressing and then heap in the
centre of the mold. Put a half pint of
mayonnaise dressing into a pastry bag
and with a star tube garnish the top of
the cream jelly and serve at once.

This may be made into individual
molds, or it may be served in paper cases,
forcing the mayonnaise over the top
through a star tube.

Cream of Tongue Salad

Chop a half pound of cold, cooked,
salt beef's tongue. Add to it a gill of
aspic jelly, a tablespoonful of lemon juice
and a saltspoonful of white pepper. Mix,
add six mushrooms chopped fine, and, if
desired, one truffle. When this begins
to stiffen stir in a half pint of good cream

which has been whipped to a stiff froth, and turn the mixture into a square pan to harden. Make it smooth and not over one inch in thickness. When cold cut into diamond-shaped pieces and arrange around a mound of mayonnaise of celery ; or, cut into rounds and place on rounds of plain aspic which have been cooled in a flat pan. Stand in nests of lettuce leaves, and garnish with mayonnaise pressed through a star tube.

Sweetbread Salad

Select a nice pair of calf's sweetbreads, wash them in cold water, throw them into boiling water, and add a teaspoonful of salt, a slice of onion, a sprig of celery and a bay leaf. Cover the saucepan and simmer gently for half an hour. Lift the sweetbreads, throw them at once into cold water. When cold pick them apart, rejecting all the membrane, and stand them away until wanted. When ready to serve rub a clove of garlic into a two-inch square crust of bread, and put it on the bottom of the salad bowl ; arrange over it the lettuce leaves. Mix the sweetbreads with mayonnaise dressing, heap them on top of the lettuce leaves and serve at once.

If this salad is served on a round or flat dish it may be garnished with pitted olives and truffles, or it may be garnished with pitted olives stuffed with mushrooms. A very pretty garnish is a row of chopped mushrooms, then a little row of finely-chopped parsley and chopped truffles sprinked over the centre.

Sweetbread and Almond Salad

Parboil the sweetbreads as directed in "Sweetbread Salad." Take them apart and stand them aside to cool. Blanch twenty-four almonds and put them in the oven until they are thoroughly dry, then chop rather fine. When ready to serve the salad cover a dish with crisp lettuce leaves, mix the almonds with the sweetbreads, add a half teaspoonful of salt, a dash of paprica, sprinkle over a tablespoonful of Worcestershire sauce, and mix thoroughly. Now mix with them a good stiff mayonnaise dressing, arrange on the lettuce leaves and serve at once.

Lobster Salad

Cut the meat from one cold boiled lobster into squares of one inch. Season with salt, pepper and lemon juice, mix with mayonnaise dressing and serve on lettuce leaves. It may be served on a round dish or in a salad bowl, or may be garnished with the shell of the lobster and lettuce leaves, the lobster rather hidden by the green.

Shrimp Salad

This is made by mixing canned or cooked shrimps with mayonnaise dressing, having first seasoned them with lemon juice, salt and pepper.

Crab Salad

Boil twelve good-sized hard crabs; pick out the meat and clean carefully seven of the nicest shells. At serving time garnish individual plates with lettuce leaves, arranging shells on the leaves. Season the meat with a teaspoonful of salt, a quarter teaspoonful of paprica and a tablespoonful of lemon juice. Mix with it a half cup of mayonnaise dressing, and heap into the crab shells, putting over each another teaspoonful of mayonnaise dressing, and dusting thickly with a mixture of chopped olives, parsley and capers ; send at once to the table.

Salmon Salad

This may be made from fresh or canned salmon. If you use fresh salmon boil it and pick it apart, rejecting the skin and bones. Arrange the bits on lettuce leaves, putting on a covering of mayonnaise dressing and serve.

Canned salmon must be turned from the can, picked apart, the oil, skin and bones rejected. Arrange the pieces on lettuce leaves with mayonnaise dressing and serve. All fish salads are better if the fish is marinated with a little lemon juice an hour before serving time.

Shad Roe Salad

Wash a shad roe, throw it into boiling water, add a teaspoonful of salt, and stand the saucepan where it cannot possibly boil for at least twenty minutes.

Lift the roe without breaking, sprinkle over it about two tablespoonfuls of tarragon vinegar and one of Worcestershire sauce, and put aside to cool. When ready to serve rub a crust of bread with garlic and put it in the centre of the dish ; put over it the lettuce leaves, arrange in the centre the shad roe cut into slices of half an inch, and cover with mayonnaise into which some whipped cream has been stirred.

Scallop Salad

Wash one pint of scallops in cold water. Cover them with boiling water and boil for five minutes. Drain and sprinkle over a tablespoonful of lemon juice, the same of Worcestershire sauce, a half tablespoonful of paprica and stand them aside. When ready to serve add a teaspoonful of salt and mix with them a half cup of mayonnaise dressing. Dish on lettuce leaves and serve immediately.

This salad may be made into a handsome dish by garnishing with pickled oyster crabs. As oyster crabs are too expensive for a salad alone they may be used as a garnish for fish salads.

Oyster Salad

Select small, plump oysters. Boil them in their own liquor until the gills are curled, then drain dry. This liquor may be used for soup. Sprinkle over the oysters two tablespoonfuls of white wine vinegar, dust over them a half teaspoonful of paprica and stand away on the ice. When ready to serve have a small jar of pickled oyster crabs and sufficient white celery cut to measure one pint to each twenty-five oysters. Have made a half pint of good mayonnaise dressing. Line a flat dish with lettuce, under which you have put a clove of garlic. Arrange the oysters in the centre of the dish. Mix with the celery a little of the mayonnaise dressing and put it around the oysters. Cover the oysters thickly with mayonnaise dressing and then cover with the drained oyster crabs. Sprinkle over the celery a little finely chopped chervil or parsley and send immediately to the table.

A plain oyster salad may be made by mixing the pickled oysters with mayonnaise dressing. They must be served immediately after the mixing.

Salads—Fruit

Cut a juicy, sour orange into thick slices. Cut it again into quarters, arrange it on lettuce leaves, cover with mayonnaise dressing and then with whipped cream.

All fruit salads may be made in the same way. White grapes are nice.

Duck in Mayonnaise

Steam a nice tame duck until tender. When cold remove the skin. Cut the meat into pieces about a half inch square and mix with it half the quantity of celery. Season with a teaspoonful of salt, a half teaspoonful of paprica, and mix with it a half pint of thick mayonnaise. Turn into a salad bowl and garnish with olives and celery tops. Serve at once.

Aspic

Cover a half box of gelatin with a half cup of cold water and soak twenty minutes. Put into a saucepan a tablespoonful of chopped carrot, the same of onion, a quarter teaspoonful of celery seed, two bay leaves, a chipping of lemon rind, a half teaspoonful of whole pepper corns, and cover with one pint of cold water. Bring to boiling point and boil five minutes. Then add a half teaspoonful of beef extract and the gelatin. Mix and strain. Beat the whites of two eggs lightly, stir them in the aspic, add the juice of one lemon and bring to a good boil. Allow it to stand a moment, and strain through two thicknesses of cheese cloth which has been wrung from cold water. Add a teaspoonful of salt, and it is ready to cool.

Chicken in Aspic

Remove the white meat from one boiled chicken and cut it into blocks. Line a mold with clear aspic. Have the lining about a quarter inch in thickness. The bottom of the mold may be garnished with truffles, mushrooms or bits of green pepper. As soon as the jelly is hard and set fill in the mold with the blocks of chicken that have been nicely seasoned. Pour over sufficient aspic to fill the spaces and stand away for at least two hours. When ready to serve garnish a round dish with lettuce leaves and turn the aspic into the centre.

Cut little red radishes into tulips, arrange them around the base of the mold and send it to the table with a good-sized boat of either plain mayonnaise or sauce tartar.

Waldorf Salad

Pare, core, quarter and slice three solid, tart apples. Cut sufficient celery to make an equal quantity. Sprinkle over a half teaspoonful of paprica, a teaspoonful of salt and a tablespoonful of lemon juice. Mix, add a cup of mayonnaise and serve at once, plain or on lettuce leaves.

Tongue in Aspic

Chop a half pound of cold boiled tongue rather fine ; add a half teaspoonful of paprica, a tablespoonful of lemon juice, one truffle chopped fine, a teaspoonful of mushroom catsup and four tablespoonfuls of aspic. Allow this to stand until it begins to stiffen, then form it into a ball. Put a very little aspic in the bottom of a plain round or bomb mold, or a small bowl may be used. Then garnish the bottom with truffles, or bits of green pepper, or both. Pour over a little more aspic to hold the garnishing. Put the ball of tongue right in the centre of the mold, pour over sufficient cold aspic to fill the mold, giving the ball shape of the mold, the space around should not be over half an inch, and filled with aspic. Stand away over night. When ready to serve turn out on a bed of cress. Cut small red radishes into slices without paring. If convenient, cut a small cucumber into slices without paring. Arrange these, over-lapping each other alternately, around the base of the mold. Send it to the table with a dish of sauce tartar.

Shred-like strips of lettuce, arranged inside the mold make an exceedingly pretty garnish. These strips are arranged with a little melted aspic. The aspic must be used cold but not congealed. Ham may be substituted for tongue, or chicken, or even beef may be used.

Sardines in Aspic

Open one box of sardines and skin them. Make a pint of aspic and pour a layer about a quarter inch thick in the bottom

of a border mold. Stand aside to harden.
When hard arrange on it, daintily, a layer
of sardines, sprinkle over a little finely-cut
cress with more jelly, which must be cold
but not congealed. When hard, put in
another layer of sardines, and fill the
mold with jelly. Stand aside to harden.
Serve with mayonnaise of celery in the
centre. Garnish with lettuce and serve.

White Aspic

Cover a quarter box of gelatin with
a quarter cup of cold water; soak a half
hour. Put in a saucepan one tablespoonful of washed butter and one of flour;
mix and add a half pint of milk. Stir
until boiling, and add a half teaspoonful
of salt, a dash of white pepper, a teaspoonful of onion juice and the gelatin.
Stir and strain. This is used as a garnish for meat salads.

Tomato Jelly

This is an exceedingly pretty and
palatable winter salad, either for lunch,
dinner or for a collation.

Cover a half box of gelatin with a

half cup of cold water; soak a half
hour. Put in a saucepan a pint of
strained tomatoes, add a stick of celery,
two bay leaves, one slice of onion. Bring
to boiling point, add the gelatin and
strain through a sieve; add a teaspoonful of salt, a tablespoonful of lemon juice,
the same of tarragon vinegar and a half
teaspoonful of paprica. Turn in small
tomato or round molds and stand aside
to harden. Serve on lettuce leaves with
mayonnaise dressing.

Mutton in White Aspic

Bone a rack of mutton and trim off
the fat. Tie in shape and put in a kettle
of boiling water ; add a bit of celery and
four bay leaves. Boil rapidly for five
minutes, then simmer gently for one
hour. Take out and cool, and when
cold cut into slices ; cut the lean meat
into rounds and season with salt and
white pepper. Have ready some white
aspic, cool but not stiff; dip in each
round of meat and lay aside to harden.
At serving time heap in the centre of a
round chop dish a mound of mayonnaise
of fringed or plain celery. Arrange the

rounds of mutton around the base, and serve. The light tops of the celery may be used as a garnish.

Pieces of chicken or filets of birds may be served the same. Both chicken and birds should be roasted.

Fringed Celery

Cut white, thick celery into two-inch lengths. Make parallel cuts on each end, then cut at right angles. Throw these into ice-water for one hour to curl. Drain and shake dry before using.

A GROUP OF ODD SALADS

A Sunday Night Salad

This is an exceedingly nice supper dish for Sunday night. The whole preparation may be done on Saturday, the dish simply garnished at serving time.

Procure a slice of halibut at least an inch and a half in thickness. Put a piece of cheese cloth into the bottom of the baking pan, lay the slice of halibut on top, sprinkle over a little chopped parsley, a chopped onion, a broken bay leaf, a half teaspoonful of celery seed, a teaspoonful of salt and a tablespoonful of lemon juice. Allow it to stand in a cool place for thirty minutes. Then place on the stove, cover with boiling water and allow it to simmer for twenty minutes. Lift the cheese cloth, carefully draining the fish. When the fish is dry turn it on the serving dish. Remove the outside skin and stand it in the refrigerator until wanted. At serving time garnish the dish with either cress or lettuce and send it to the table. Pass with it a boat of sauce tartar or cooked mayonnaise sauce.

Fish Creams

Rub fine bits of cold boiled fish with the back of a spoon. To each half pint of this mixture allow two tablespoonfuls of thick cream, a tablespoonful or an eighth of a box of gelatin, a tablespoonful of lemon juice, a teaspoonful of salt, twenty-four chopped almonds and a quarter teaspoonful of pepper. Cover the gelatin with two tablespoonfuls of cold water; allow it to soak. Then stand it over the tea-kettle until thoroughly melted. Add all the seasonings and the cream to the fish and stir in the gelatin. Allow this mixture to stand until partly congealed, then moisten the hands with cold water, and roll a tablespoonful of the mixture into a ball. Stand these balls aside until cold and hard. At serving time arrange little nests of lettuce leaves; in the centre of each put a slice of pickled beet, and on top and in the centre of this stand one of the little balls. Make a stiff mayonnaise dressing, and add to it a tablespoonful of melted gelatin. When it begins to congeal stir in about three table-spoonfuls of stiffly whipped cream. Put this mixture in a pastry bag containing a small star tube. Decorate the top of the ball and then make a rope-like decoration around the edge of the beet, allowing the mayonnaise to touch the edge of the beet, but resting upon the lettuce leaves. Send at once to the table.

The beauty of the dish lies in having this pink showing at the bottom of the ball. A single caper may be placed on top of each ball; or the balls may be covered all over with mayonnaise dressing, then decorated in fancy forms with capers.

Japanese Salad

Throw a half cup of rice into a kettle of boiling water and boil rapidly for thirty minutes; then drain and stand aside to dry. Put a half teaspoonful of salt, a quarter teaspoonful of pepper and six tablespoonfuls of oil into a bowl; mix thoroughly and add a tablespoonful of finely shredded onion and two tablespoonfuls of vinegar. Pour this over the hot rice, mix, and stand aside until cold. When ready to serve, cover a round dish with either lettuce or cress and turn the salad into the centre, forming it into a mound. Around the base of this mound put in a swimming position twelve sardines. Pare a red beet, then with a knife pare the flesh around and around until it is a long ribbon-like piece. Roll this up compactly and with a knife slice it down from the end as if cutting down a roll of noodles. Throw into cold water for at least thirty minutes. Shake perfectly dry, put this thread-like beet all over the top of the rice, and send immediately to the table.

Russian Salad

Pick apart half of a small boiled mackerel. Put it into a bowl. Add to it sufficient cold cooked beef, cut into blocks, to make a half pint. Pare and cut into thin slices one cucumber. Add two boiled potatoes cut into dice, then a tablespoonful of capers, six olives cut into eighths, and two sardines broken apart. Mix carefully and sprinkle over two tablespoonfuls of tarragon vinegar, a half teaspoonful of salt, a quarter teaspoonful of paprica, and a tablespoonful of finely-chopped onion. Stand aside for one or two hours. At serving time, line your salad bowl with lettuce leaves. Put into a bowl a half teaspoonful of salt, a quarter teaspoonful of white pepper, and add gradually six tablespoonfuls of oil ; mix ; add a tablespoonful of tarragon vinegar ; mix again, and add the pulp of one small orange or half a shaddock. Turn this over the other mixture, dish on the lettuce leaves and serve at once.

Herring Salad

Cut four cold boiled potatoes into thin slices. Pare and cut the same way two tart apples. Cut into bits two pickled herring. Cut into dice sufficient cold roast beef to make a half pint. Mix all these together and add a tablespoonful of finely-chopped onion, a quarter teaspoonful of celery seeds, a tablespoonful of tarragon vinegar, and stand them in the refrigerator until wanted. At serving time line the dish with lettuce or cress. Put into a bowl a teaspoonful of salt, a quarter teaspoonful of pepper and six tablespoonfuls of oil. Rub until the salt is dissolved ; then add a tablespoonful of lemon juice and a tablespoonful of vinegar. Mix thoroughly and stir in a teaspoonful of Worcestershire sauce, and a teaspoonful of German made mustard. Pour this over the meat mixture, place on the lettuce leaves and serve at once.

Egg Salad

Put six eggs into warm water; bring them to boiling point and simmer gently for fifteen minutes. Cool, remove the shells and cut the eggs into slices. Arrange these slices, overlapping each other, in the centre of a dish which has been lined with lettuce leaves. Sprinkle over some finely-chopped parsley, cover with French dressing which has been seasoned with a half teaspoonful of German mustard, and serve at once.

A Summer Salad

Cut radishes without paring into slices. Pare and cut a good-sized cucumber into slices and slice two solid tomatoes. Cut three cold boiled potatoes into blocks, and mix with them Sidney Smith's salad dressing. Heap them in the centre of a dish and finish with alternate layers of cucumber, tomato and radishes, the slices overlapping each other. Chop sufficient parsley to make about two tablespoonfuls and put a little row of this around the edge of the dish. Pour over the vegetables a little French dressing and serve at once.

CEYLON SALADS

These salads are not served as a regular dinner salad; that is, they do not form a course, but are usually served as an accompaniment to cold roast beef or mutton. The cream should be made the day before it is wanted.

Cocoanut Cream

Grate one good-sized cocoanut, and pour over it a pint of boiling water. Wash and stir until all the goodness has been washed from the fibre. Turn this into a cheese cloth and press it firmly. Stand the milk thus obtained aside over night, and by morning a good thick cream will have formed on the surface. Remove this and put it aside for use. The milk underneath may be used for sauces of various kinds.

Ceylon Tomato Salad

Peel three solid tomatoes, cut them into halves and press out the seeds.

L. of C.

Chop the flesh of the tomato rather fine. Put it into a bowl, add a tablespoonful of lemon juice, a level teaspoonful of salt, a tablespoonful of chopped onion, the same of chopped green sweet pepper, and a half teaspoonful of paprica. Mix and turn into the dish in which it is to be served. Stir cocoanut cream until to the consistency of very thick cream. Pour four tablespoonfuls over the tomatoes and send to the table.

Ceylon Cucumber Salad

This is one of the daintiest of all salads to serve with fish. It may be used as a sauce for deviled fish or any fish served in individual shells.

Pare three good-sized cucumbers ; cut into halves and remove the seeds. Chop the cucumber fine, add to it a teaspoonful of salt, a tablespoonful of lemon juice and the same of onion juice. Dish, pour over cocoanut cream and send to the table.

Celery and Pepper Salad

This salad, like other Ceylon salads, is served as an accompaniment to a meat dish. It is exceedingly nice to serve with chicken croquettes or chicken cutlets.

Chop fine sufficient celery to make a half pint; add to it one green sweet pepper chopped fine, a half teaspoonful of salt, a tablespoonful of lemon juice, a tablespoonful of onion juice; a half teaspoonful of paprica, and a table-spoonful of finely-chopped green ginger. If the green ginger cannot be obtained sprinkle over a quarter teaspoonful of dry ginger. Dish the mixture. Pour over the cream from one cocoanut and send to the table.

Ceylon Cauliflower Salad

Boil one sound head of cauliflower and break it apart in flowerets. Sprinkle over the juice of one lemon, two table-spoonfuls of onion juice, a half teaspoon-ful of paprica, and stand aside until wanted. At serving time line a round dish with lettuce leaves. Put into a bowl a half teaspoonful of salt, two table-spoonfuls of lemon juice and a half tea-spoonful of curry powder. Mix thor-oughly and stir in the cream from one

cocoanut. Pour this over the cauliflower and send at once to the table.
This salad may be served as a salad
course.

By using a little ingenuity and chang-
ing the vegetables one may make a great
variety of these beautiful salads. The
principal seasonings will be lemon juice,
pepper, ginger and onion juice, with a
covering of the cocoanut cream.

INDEX